TO:

_____

FROM:

_____

Text © 2014 Thomas S. Monson
Illustrations © 2014 Dan Burr
Art direction by Richard Erickson
Design by Sheryl Dickert Smith

Visit us at ShadowMountain.com

Library of Congress Cataloging-in-Publication Data
ISBN 978-1-60907-868-3
(CIP data on file)

Printed in the United States of America
Publishers Printing, Salt Lake City, UT

10 9 8 7 6 5 4 3 2 1

01/2014

One Little Match

THOMAS S. MONSON

ILLUSTRATED BY DAN BURR

SHADOW
MOUNTAIN

When I was growing up, each summer from early July until early September my family stayed at our cabin at Vivian Park in Provo Canyon in Utah.

One of my best friends during those carefree days was Danny Larsen, whose family also owned a cabin at Vivian Park. Every day he and I roamed this children's paradise to find the best spot on the river to fish.

Besides catching fish, we collected rocks from the stream or found other treasures, like an empty bird's nest or a discarded antler. It was even fun to find dead bugs for my bug collection.

There were always plenty of trails to hike and trees to climb. Danny and I enjoyed each minute of each hour of each day.

One morning, as we sat on the cabin steps, Danny asked, "What should we do today, Tommy?"

I thought about all the possibilities. Suddenly, I had a new thought. With a bit of excitement, I said, "We should have a campfire tonight with all of our canyon friends!"

"Great idea!" Danny said. "But we'll need to clear a space big enough for all of us to fit."

"I know just the field," I smiled.

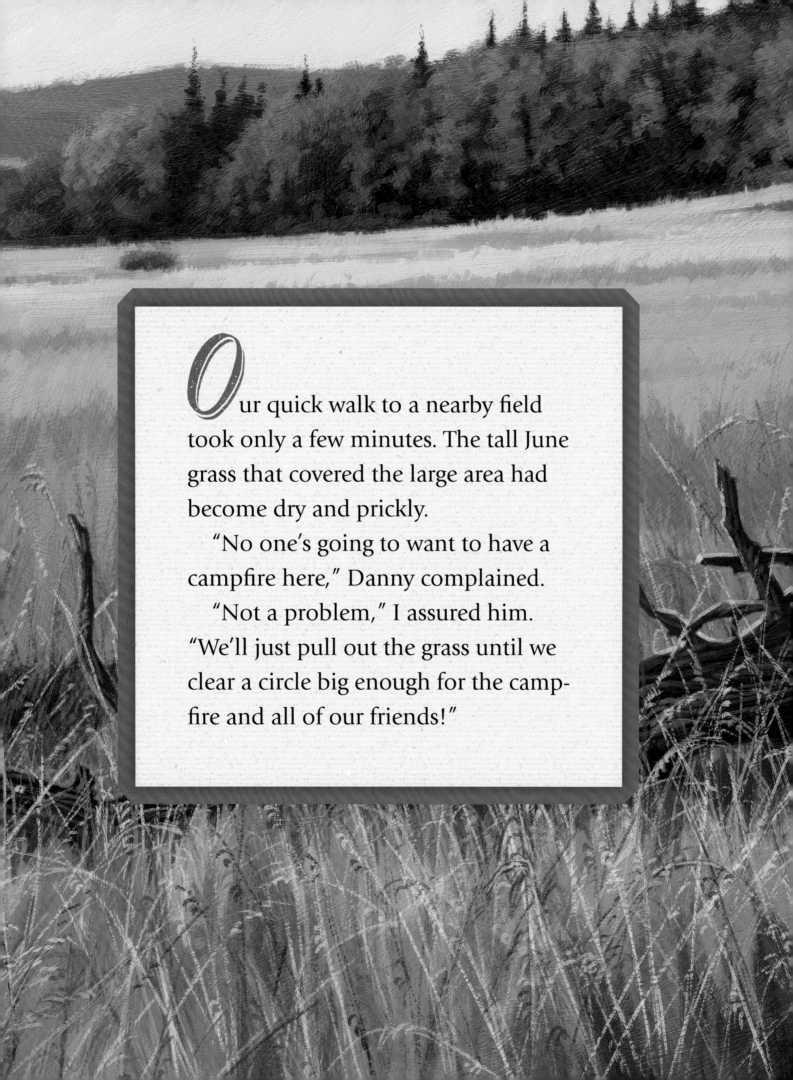

Our quick walk to a nearby field took only a few minutes. The tall June grass that covered the large area had become dry and prickly.

"No one's going to want to have a campfire here," Danny complained.

"Not a problem," I assured him. "We'll just pull out the grass until we clear a circle big enough for the campfire and all of our friends!"

We began to pull at the tall grass, but our enthusiasm didn't last long. We tugged and yanked with all our might, but all we got were small handfuls of the stubborn weeds.

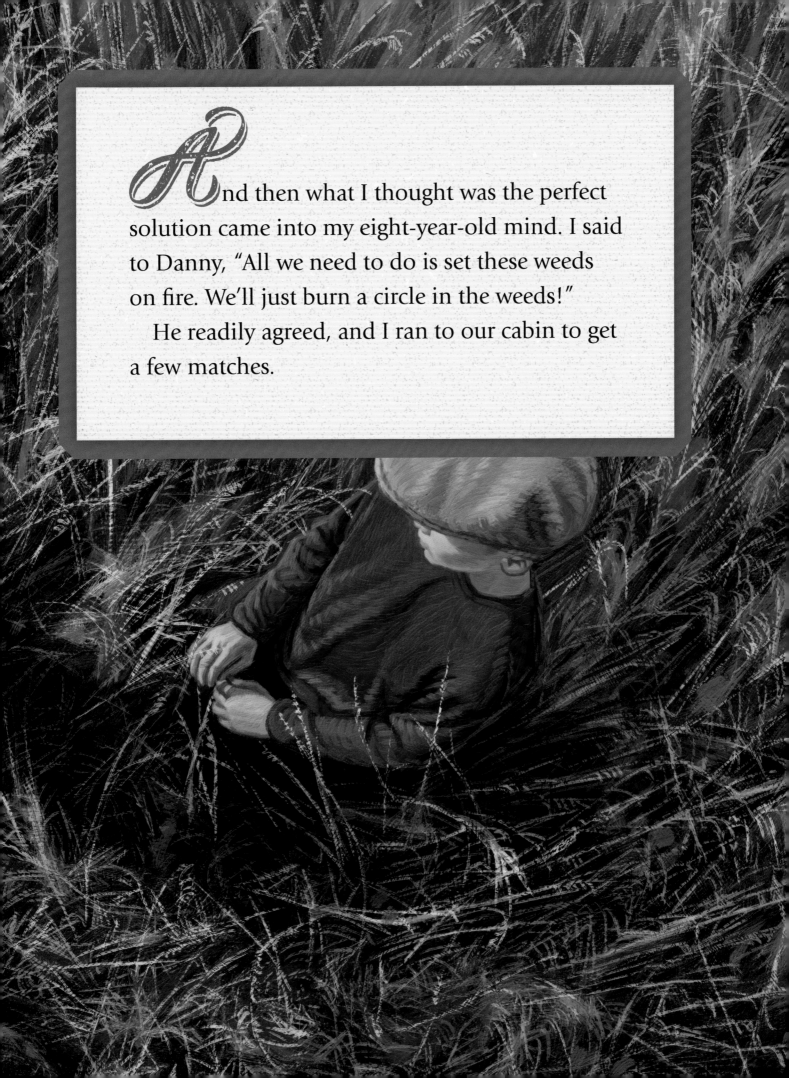

*A*nd then what I thought was the perfect solution came into my eight-year-old mind. I said to Danny, "All we need to do is set these weeds on fire. We'll just burn a circle in the weeds!"

He readily agreed, and I ran to our cabin to get a few matches.

For one little moment, I remembered the many lessons that my parents had taught me about the danger of fire. In fact, at the young age of eight I wasn't even permitted to use matches without adult supervision. However, Danny and I needed to clear the field, and using a match would be the fastest way to do it. Without even a second thought, I ignored the warning and found the box of matches in the kitchen. I grabbed a few matchsticks, making certain no one was watching, and quickly hid them in one of my pockets.

$\mathcal{B}$ack to Danny I ran, excited that in my hand was the answer to our problem. I recall thinking that the fire would burn only as far as we wanted and then would somehow magically extinguish itself.

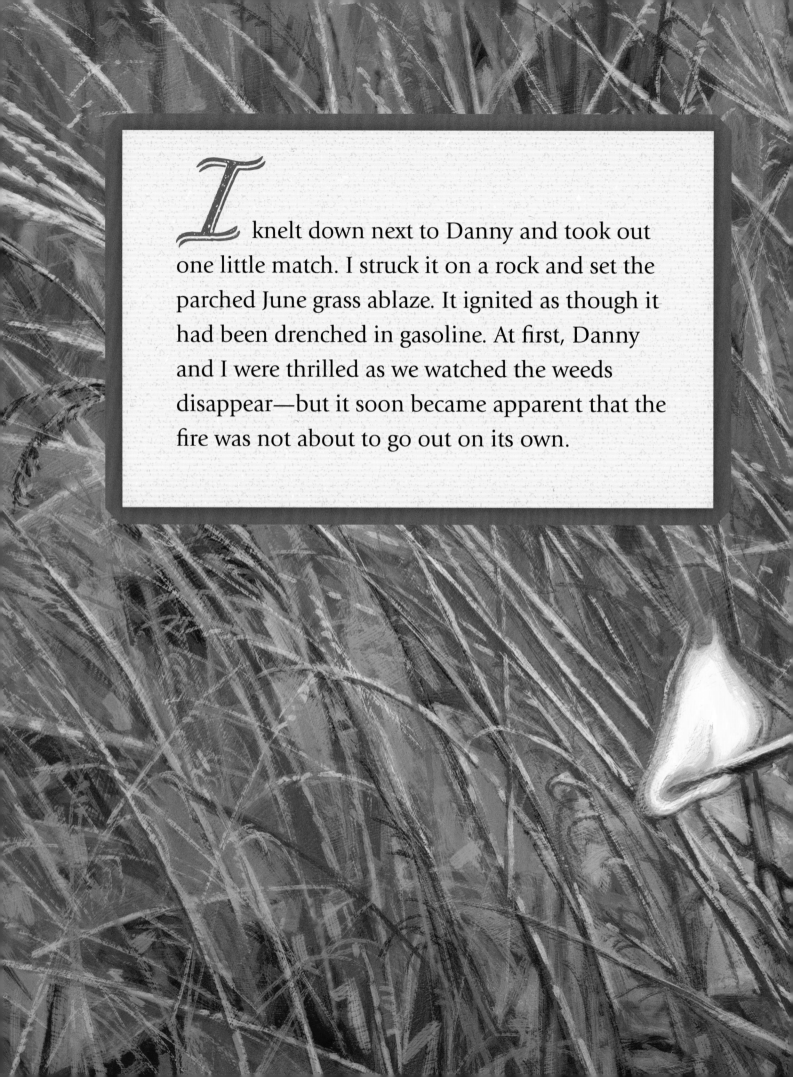

$\mathcal{I}$ knelt down next to Danny and took out one little match. I struck it on a rock and set the parched June grass ablaze. It ignited as though it had been drenched in gasoline. At first, Danny and I were thrilled as we watched the weeds disappear—but it soon became apparent that the fire was not about to go out on its own.

We panicked as we realized there was nothing we could do to stop the blaze. The menacing flames began to follow the wild grass up the mountainside, endangering the pine trees and everything else in their path.

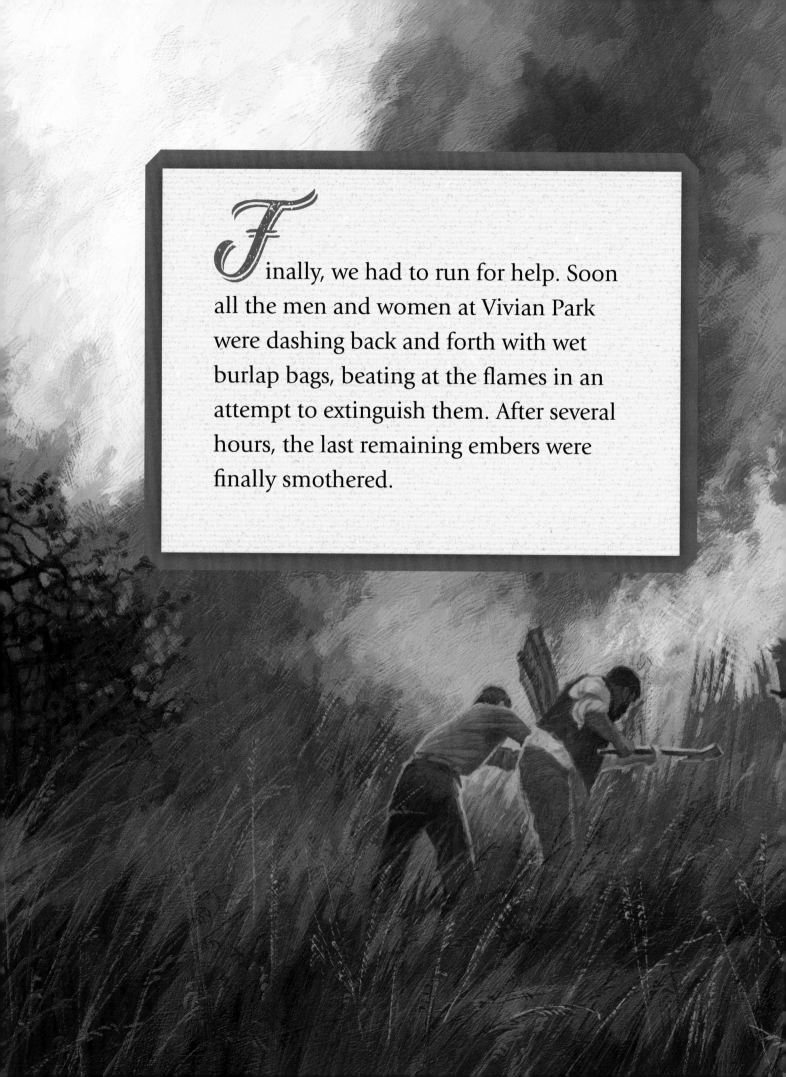

Finally, we had to run for help. Soon all the men and women at Vivian Park were dashing back and forth with wet burlap bags, beating at the flames in an attempt to extinguish them. After several hours, the last remaining embers were finally smothered.

anny and I were exhausted and humbled. We felt terrible about what had happened. If only I had acted differently in that one little second and never picked up even one little match.

I learned several difficult but important lessons that day. Perhaps the biggest lesson was the need for obedience. Rules and laws are created to keep us safe. When we obey those rules, we can avoid the dangers that can come from something as small as one little match.

The Lord our God will we serve,
and his voice will we obey.

–JOSHUA 24:24